TIME'S ORIEL

Poetry by the same author

COLLECTIONS
The Rain-Giver
The Dream-House

SELECTION
Between My Father and My Son

LIMITED EDITIONS
On Approval
My Son
Alderney: The Nunnery
Norfolk Poems
Petal and Stone

TRANSLATIONS
The Battle of Maldon and Other Old English Poems
Beowulf
The Exeter Book Riddles

TIME'S ORIEL
Poems by Kevin Crossley-Holland

Hutchinson
London Melbourne Sydney Auckland Johannesburg

Hutchinson & Co. (Publishing) Ltd
An imprint of the Hutchinson Publishing Group
17–21 Conway Street, London W1P 6JD

Hutchinson Group (Australia) Pty Ltd
30–32 Cremorne Street, Richmond South, Victoria 3121
PO Box 151, Broadway, New South Wales 2007

Hutchinson Group (NZ) Ltd
32–34 View Road, PO Box 40–086, Glenfield, Auckland 10

Hutchinson Group (SA) (Pty) Ltd
PO Box 337, Bergvlei 2012, South Africa

First published 1983
© Kevin Crossley-Holland 1983

Set in Sabon by D. P. Media Limited, Hitchin, Hertfordshire
Printed in Great Britain by The Anchor Press Ltd
and bound by Wm Brendon & Son Ltd
both of Tiptree, Essex

British Library Cataloguing in Publication Data

Crossley-Holland, Kevin
  Time's oriel.
  I. Title
  821'.914   PR6053.R/
ISBN 0 09 153291 4

for my sons
Kieran and Dominic

Contents

Acknowledgements   8
The Monk's Reflections   9
Wulf   12
In the Midst of Life   13
Children in the Cherry Tree   14
Grandmother's Footsteps   15
Mimesis   16
The Wanderer   17
Night Flight Out of England   21
Germanic Snapshots   22
A Bavarian Miscellany   24
Beyond this Boundary   28
In a Suburban Museum   29
A Small Ritual   30
Catalogue   31
The Angel Tree   32
The Echoing Stile   33
At Fiesole   34
An Approach to the Marsh   35
The Old Apple-Tree   36
Mary   37
Place of Pilgrimage   38
In Dorset and Wiltshire   39
Postcards from Kodai   40
Mosquito   42
Three Ways of Pinking Ivory   43
Note on the Language Riots in Tamil Nadu, 1967   44
South-West Monsoon   45
At St Gregory's Minster, Kirkdale   47
Neenie   48
After Your Death   50
A Wreath   51
Cassandra   52
Dragon   54
Deliverance   55
Death and the Maiden   56
If Only the Wind   60
Moon-Child   61

Acknowledgements

Thanks are due to the editors of the following magazines in which most of these poems first appeared: *Agenda, Encounter, The Listener, The Literary Half-Yearly, The New Statesman, Outposts, The Poetry Review, Samphire, The Tablet* and *The Times Literary Supplement*.

'Grandmother's Footsteps' was broadcast on 'Poetry Now' (Radio 3). 'The Echoing Stile' was broadcast by BBC Schools in the 'Living Language' series and first printed by BBC Publications. 'Mosquito' and 'Postcards from Kodai' were broadcast by All India Radio, and 'In a Suburban Museum' by WUOM/WVGR Public Radio Station.

'Deliverance' has been printed in *Night Ride and Sunrise*, edited by Edward Lowbury.

Seven poems first appeared in *Between My Father and My Son*, published by the Black Willow Press (USA).

The Monk's Reflections

Too much consistency: at last I dared
Kick the comfortable restraints, the bells'
Gentle hubbub, fraternal silences,
Dispersals and reunions. All our
Observances, the Rule, had become soft
With regiment and custom: time to change.

This is what I tried to think, partly thought,
Repeated so often because I had
Still to convince myself; then I kissed all
My brethren and under my skin hurried
To the spines of breakers, growling and grey-green,
The bucking ocean. My heart was aching.

I wanted to negotiate my own
Way to heaven, a crash course hazardous
With iceberg and whale: glass mountains that sing
Of how they will mother what mothered them;
Fastitocalon, apparent island
Who sinks the unwary anchored on him.

So for love I sailed north. Guided by God,
Wind-guardian, I left the secret glades,
The salmon streams, and crossed the bitter sea
Until I was driven to this loveless
Extremity. And, even now, I do
Not know the name of this icy cauldron.

This is my cell of the senses: time counts
In here and I count it – for each day
One stroke on that stripped log, and each full moon
A striation. My knife itself is pared
Like bark or rind. Five years, and rows of days...
Only God can tell how many longer.

And in that small cell, with its sky-ceiling,
I celebrate the offices. *O God,*
Seven times a day do I praise thee. At
Midnight I will rise and give thanks to thee.
Between boulders I pray, and between
Prayers cultivate crops and fantasies.

For how can I forget her, Grania,
Her flaming eyes? I cannot help my dreams.
I'm a rack-wretch, even now unable
To forget her, unable to flatten
The mind's fenders and remember clearly.
Even these words . . . .

Your voice had to do with the bees; your eyes
Were on fire. Do you think of that green glade,
The sun behind the leaves, the leafy bed?
Do you think about those oaths, made and broken?
How did you look? And how do you look now,
Your oval face I saw in every face,

From which, after all, there is no escape?
I thought it was right to come, and maybe
It was right, but I should have explained it.
At least that. Now I cannot undo it,
And even if in time you understood,
You will have branded me lover-coward.

Life around me as my body withers:
The timeless stream of all things that are born
And do die, all children of one mother.
I am peaceful at times, incorporate;
Then the sublime whole shatters, and each part
Translates her, it embodies Grania.

I single out a sweet pattern of stars,
Her configuration in the chill air,
She is that remote light on the mountain,
This brown-eyed flower. Each is an ambush,
A torturer divine; for though I live –
In labour, prayer, shifting dream – I seem now

To live only through these incarnations.

Wulf
a retranslation from Old English

Prey, it's as if my people have been handed prey.
They'll tear him to pieces if he comes with a troop.

O, we are apart.

Wulf is on one island, I on another,
a fastness that island, a fen-prison.
Fierce men roam there, on that island;
they'll tear him to pieces if he comes with a troop.

O, we are apart.

How I have grieved for my Wulf's wide wanderings.
When rain slapped the earth and I sat apart weeping,
when the bold warrior wrapped his arms about me,
I seethed with desire and yet with such hatred.
Wulf, my Wulf, my yearning for you
and your seldom coming have caused my sickness,
my mourning heart, not mere starvation.
Can you hear, Eadwacer? Wulf will spirit
our pitiful whelp to the woods.
Men easily savage what was never secure,
our song together.

In the Midst of Life

He will not outlive that last leavetaking.
Morning and maybe she was dressed in blue
And in her face he thought he saw she knew
The dragon's teeth were of their joint sowing
And must accept, and soon, that his going
Mattered less than the cause and the waking.

Morning and she stood at the huge window,
An English Christ-child in her arms, white-haired
And grave and knowing; unmoving he stared
And both – all three – seemed aware of what must
Come, what suffering spring where love and trust
Should grow. He tore himself apart to go

And will not outlive that last leavetaking,
Buried in him as in them, still waking, slow.

Children in the Cherry Tree

They perch in the cherry tree — two fledglings
Not quite hidden, gigglers in the dusk, hatching a plan.
The tree begins to shake them. It is not laughing,
It groans, its limbs beat slowly like prehistoric wings
And skin-soft leaves, yellow and pink and red, cascade.

So high and so cold, the tree now such a stranger.

Peering out from their eyrie, and down through the web
Of branches, the silent high-riders hear shouts
In their throats. Their colours are lowered, dashes
Of scarlet and white legging it down as light fails,
As darkness lopes along the waiting blue hills.

Grandmother's Footsteps

No to the birds no to the flowers no to the sprinkler
All washing the garden with soft water colours
As the sun goes down. No to the friends presents
Cakes candles laughter. It is as if they were not
And had never been. Alone she stands at one end
Of the lawn facing all that does not matter
Only aware of that dark tunnel behind her.

As the shapes approach stealthy and insistent
Steps of the smilers silent and murderous
She clenches her teeth her fists her limbs almost lock
And she stares into the darkness. But there
Is still so much she can do with sheer vigilance
For so long for as long as her mind body her own will
Do not work against her. There! And there!
In her straitjacket she jerks twists round
'You and you and Ivan you Sally and you
I saw you moving almost all of you.'
Laughing they troop back to the starting-line most of them
But no not all those other ones how long will it be?

The garden is hushed at sundown it is breathless
And the blooms burn to ashes. She knows they must get her
In the end they must let that be soon now.
As if only it were not a deadly serious game
How gladly she would let the first last shape touch her
And even embrace it weeping from such weariness
And relief. But as it is she turns and turns . . . .

Mimesis

Nothing much moves; nothing that moves is up to any good.
There's little to be said for getting lost in this wood
That was afternoon-subtle, a kind of gentle accompanist
Now turned unfriendly, an inescapable catalyst
Of dark anxieties. This comes of too much burning:
My son, you've been with me at every thoughtless turning.

Now to whistle or warble or gargle like a bird
Settling in for the night, a snatch in the darkness
To keep my pecker up, is to do as you do, conjuror
With finches, small attendant of small colonies
That settle beside you, sharing your confidence.

To stick my hands into my pockets as an assertion
Of some kind of self-reliance, a show only for myself
Of nonchalance, is to do as you do, in so far
As you can find room among penknife, sweets, string,
A wishbone, conkers, coins, your complete survival kit.

Yes, to look around carefully and see the dark shapes
Are only dark shapes, and yet feel the inexorable pressure
Of night, is to do as you do, enviable at least
In that you are a fighter, realist perhaps too soon
Who knows when to use and when refuse imagination.

I say how poised you are, and that is right.
But that dark .... At each separation you duck, hurtle out of sight,
Eyes fearful. You know I know, and knowing care:
You will not break with more show your necessary barrier.
Expression is not always words. I stand, unready to shout,
Equally unready to accept there's no way out.

The Wanderer
a translation from Old English

Often the wanderer pleads for pity
and mercy from the Lord; but for a long time,
sad in mind, he must dip his oars
into icy waters, the lanes of the sea;
he must follow the paths of exile: fate is inflexible.

Mindful of hardships, grievous slaughter,
the ruin of kinsmen, the wanderer said:
'Time and again at the day's dawning
I must mourn all my afflictions alone.
There is no one still living to whom I dare open
the doors of my heart. I have no doubt
that it is a noble habit for a man
to bind fast all his heart's feelings,
guard his thoughts, whatever he is thinking.
The weary in spirit cannot withstand fate,
and nothing comes of venting spleen:
wherefore those eager for glory often
hold some ache imprisoned in their hearts.
Thus I had to bind my feelings in fetters,
often sad at heart, cut off from my country,
far from my kinsmen, after, long ago,
dark clods of earth covered my gold-friend;
I left that place in wretchedness,
ploughed the icy waves with winter in my heart;
in sadness I sought far and wide
for a treasure-giver, for a man
who would welcome me into his mead-hall,
give me good cheer (for I boasted no friends),
entertain me with delights. He who has experienced it
knows how cruel a comrade sorrow can be
to any man who has few loyal friends:
for him are the ways of exile, in no wise twisted gold;
for him is a frozen body, in no wise the fruits of the earth.
He remembers hall-retainers and treasure
and how, in his youth, his gold-friend
entertained him. Those joys have all vanished.

A man who lacks advice for a long while
from his loved lord understands this,
that when sorrow and sleep together
hold the wretched wanderer in their grip,
it seems that he clasps and kisses
his lord, and lays hands and head
upon his lord's knee as he had sometimes done
when he enjoyed the gift-throne in earlier days.
Then the friendless man wakes again
and sees the dark waves surging around him,
the sea-birds bathing, spreading their feathers,
frost and snow falling mingled with hail.

Then his wounds lie more heavy in his heart,
aching for his lord. His sorrow is renewed;
the memory of kinsmen sweeps through his mind;
joyfully he welcomes them, eagerly scans
his comrade warriors. Then they swim away again.
Their drifting spirits do not bring many old songs
to his lips. Sorrow upon sorrow attend
the man who must send time and again
his weary heart over the frozen waves.

And thus I cannot think why in the world
my mind does not darken when I brood on the fate
of brave warriors, how they have suddenly
had to leave the mead-hall, the bold followers.
So this world dwindles day by day,
and passes away; for a man will not be wise
before he has weathered his share of winters
in the world. A wise man must be patient,
neither too passionate nor too hasty of speech,
neither too irresolute nor too rash in battle;
not too anxious, too content, nor too grasping,
and never too eager to boast before he knows himself.
When he boasts a man must bide his time
until he has no doubt in his brave heart
that he has fully made up his mind.

A wise man must fathom how eerie it will be
when all the riches of the world stand waste,
as now in diverse places in this middle-earth
walls stand, tugged at by winds
and hung with hoar-frost, building in decay.
The wine-halls crumble, lords lie dead,
deprived of joy, all the proud followers
have fallen by the wall: battle carried off some,
led them on journeys; the bird carried one
over the welling waters; one the grey wolf
devoured; a warrior with downcast face
hid one in an earth-cave.
Thus the Maker of Men laid this world waste
until the ancient works of the giants stood idle,
hushed without the hubbub of inhabitants.

Then he who has brooded over these noble ruins,
and who deeply ponders this dark life,
wise in his mind, often remembers
the many slaughters of the past and speaks these words:
Where has the horse gone? Where the man? Where the giver of gold?
Where is the feasting-place? And where the pleasures of the hall?
I mourn the gleaming cup, the warrior in his corselet,
the glory of the prince. How that time has passed away,
darkened under the shadow of night as if it had never been.
Where the loved warriors were, there now stands a wall
of wondrous height, carved with serpent forms.
The savage ash-spears, avid for slaughter,
have claimed all the warriors – a glorious fate!
Storms crash against these rocky slopes,
sleet and snow fall and fetter the world,
winter howls, then darkness draws on,
the night-shadow casts gloom and brings
fierce hailstorms from the north to frighten men.
Nothing is ever easy in the kingdom of earth,
the world beneath the heavens is in the hands of fate.
Here possessions are fleeting, here friends are fleeting,

here man is fleeting, here kinsman is fleeting,
the whole world becomes a wilderness.

So spoke the wise man in his heart as he sat apart in thought.
Brave is the man who holds to his beliefs; nor shall he ever
show the sorrow in his heart before he knows how he
can hope to heal it. It is best for a man to seek
mercy and comfort from the Father in heaven where security
    stands for us all.

Night Flight Out of England

Already alien: a shining pictograph I can't decipher.
And then a gold settlement not quite as regular
As polka dots; solitaries like stars fallen,
Or just night lights on landings, so dim and forever;
Spokes shooting from a hub that's greenish and ethereal,
Tangents, rhomboids, all that matter made material;
And then the last arrested flash, a scimitar of light,
And I am in the dark; and rising still, still rising,
Quickening to prospects beyond the darkness, look back
Almost lovingly at the land's concealed depressions,
Those seeming patterns, the whole bright bag of tricks.

Germanic Snapshots
for Gundi Kübler

Aged three, a page in gold satin trousers
Is caught in a frieze: casual from habit
The concertina breathes again and sings
In the afterblast; the wedding breakfast
Continues.
        One food parcel on parade
At Adcock and Percival – squads of tins,
And size 12 black shoes. 'For a family,'
The woman says, 'who are hungry and poor.
They live in Germany.'
                Lake of Lucerne:
In a pedal-boat a little boy howls,
And an anxious woman calls from the bank.
But the man releases one small trapped foot
And pushes forward on his pilgrimage,
Bent on reaching Triebschen.
                      Fafnir bellows,
He moves like a juggernaut. Sheer gold-lust:
Self-made monster! Yet his body contains
Such wells of understanding, the same veins
Knotted with brutality.
                On the baize
Mock O-Level results. Mocking display!
GERMAN. *Crossley-Holland, K. 3%*
Advised not to sit exam.
                    At his heart
He wears her picture, love's insignia,
Inscribed Steffi. Vergissmeinnicht. No good.
He has quite forgotten, inert amongst
The gunpit spoil, sprawling under the sun.
And reading of this in controlled grave words,
A student for the first time apprehends
Love's force, the force of war, and time defused
By a poem.
        Wena me þina
Seoce gedydon, þine seldcymas,
Murnende mod . . . .
                  Passenger in transit,

Slumped in an airport lounge. He is dreaming,
You can tell that. Links, associations?
The long stalk and common root? His eyes film.
He will make proper sense of this journey.

A Bavarian Miscellany

The Danube in Spate: Regensburg

Hunches its shoulders, butts,
roars with seven voices

under the arches

of the bridge that rises
and vaults like a leaping deer.

Rhein-Main-Donau Kanal

Charlemagne's dream, Ludwig I's scheme,
endorsed by the Bundestag, irreversible. . . .
Where's the rhyme in the tearing down
of willows and the bastions of concrete,
Altmühltal broken and reset?
I do not see the end; I see there
is no end; I see the end.
Inside every good German
is another concrete-mixer!

Elbow-Wrestling in the Beer Tent

You will remember what? I remember
the bonhomie, smell of sweat,
the beer and shimmer of heat,
and the mandatory raucous singing,
'Ein Prosit! Ein Prosit! Der Gemütlichkeit!'
Remember one arm, hairy, muscular,
and your own, white and shot
with gold hair? Your forearm
not half the length of his
as you planted your elbow
on the trestle table, grinned
and, sticking out your chin, grasped hands.

Snowfall

Six inches last night!
Under the white and shining blanket
shoulders heave, eaves drip
already, trills cascade
from the swaying fir;
the shovellers are out
cutting through this fallen flesh,
sweating, scraping the pavement.

An Indian Explains

The bishop was a lily
in his last incarnation.

His face is a waxen
spathe. Is he not stately?

Look at his pointed fingers.
And consider his liver.

Sunday Morning: Fürstenfeldbruck

Far-off humming. Or not even a humming,
just a mild vibration the ear registers
as different from the wash of cool spring air.
But then, in lulls irregular when even the drift
pauses and hangs like a creek tide on the turn,
you can make out the colours, overlapping
and never quite distinct, of half-a-dozen
belfries of distant, free-swinging bells.

München HBF, Friday in March, 18.00

Into the arms of loved ones
the travellers tumble. There are no barriers,
the whole platform hums with weekend reunions.

This year, next year, sometime . . . .
Remember the ache of early spring?
The train for Florence at 23.15?

No! Neither north nor south, east nor west
can bring him closer to her.

Intransigence: Piano Practice

Jon. Seb. Bach: Praeludium I.
The girl bends over the keys
and all she sees is black and white
and the wall, the waterfall of her hair.

Regensburg

From somewhere smoke drifts . . .
                                      it wafts
across the face of each building
(as this morning, mist cased each hollow
and swathed the banks of the Danube).

She sleeps . . .
              in the locked churches
the cherubs smile cherubic smiles
and, under the Dom, the radish-seller engraved
by Bartlett dozes in the sunlight.

And waits . . .
           too old to be impatient,
history heavy on her shoulders
(like snow on the shoulders of the Salzstadl),
for the next or the last clarion call.

Coda

We could have met, an insurance unrealized.

Home, love's loss comes home at last,
the miles become measurable . . . .

As before, uncertain foghorns sound
on the river, coathangers quietly rock

in the bedroom wardrobe. What is there
that here and now I do not remember?

Not yet, not yet the call of my neighbour.

Beyond this Boundary

Beyond this boundary, my friend,
there are no maps no roads
and from the spellbound hamlet
in the forest clearing – seventeen houses
silent and expectant, antlers raised
over doorposts – there is no return.

I live there still. In the schloss
the dancing feet are silent.
A single monk, aged eighty-eight, brother
of the duke, lives alone in splendour.
He lets down a key in a bucket.
Pray where does this lead to?

At Friedenstrasse 13, the dead
sleep under a voltage of bluebells;
it is always time for vespers.
Beyond the seven piers and the river
rush, the cathedral sparrows
sing Monteverdi. Madly o madly.

These are ley lines. Also
the magic flute and the song
of the woodbird; seven deer concealed
in the field of swaying corn;
the lady on the lonely hill
remembering a former time.

Time's wind bristles. But what
is left in its wake is stubborn
and persistent: emblems
of an undying enchantment.
Only keep your head well down
alert for the telltale signs.

In a Suburban Museum

They have withdrawn the exhibit with two left feet,
A scowling Anglo-Saxon not feeling quite himself.
His pins were his only present claim to fame
And they have been taken from under him. This man
Is used to waiting, though; in time he may be dusted
And labelled, *Early Victim of a Bureaucratic Muddle*.

The irreverent *lof* we visit on you is only worse
If you were a man not to tangle with – a harpist,
An athlete or weaver with a price on your limbs.
Take these words as *wergild*, as I take yours,
Hoarse and passionate, echoing still and always
In time's oriel, and love you for them: *Bone to bone,
Blood to blood, limb to limb, thus they are fitted together.*
Wherever you are now, *freond*, put your best foot forward.

A Small Ritual

Five young ladies with their butts in the air
Each bent on finding one fossilized vertebra
On the weird waste island of Lindisfarne

Cuthbert's bead is a passport to come back
They know the story but want the knack
On the weird waste island of Lindisfarne

Are they aware that those in ritual's pay
Keep the dragon of anarchy at bay
On the weird waste island of Lindisfarne

This is the Anglo-Saxon legacy
Passion for order and for ceremony
On the weird waste island of Lindisfarne

Five students, five Marxists, five pretty rumps
But not one echinoderm to give them the jumps
On the weird waste island of Lindisfarne

Catalogue

The shape of her face: oval. So these shows begin.
Now her eyes, her nose, her mouth; advance to her chin;
The nape of her neck (and the colour of her skin),

The stance of her shoulders; so proceed to those breasts . . . .
Ah, that game! Stop-at-nothing, ceremonious,
Observed still by this poet and medievalist.

The Angel Tree

One has a tongue of fire
And one has a small mouth and the murmur of a dove

Promises promises promises
I will keep them if I can one says

One professes to know the secrets of silent places
The oak groves bearing mistletoe
Circles of gaunt stones

One has such energy she shines as if in armour

One is a boulder unmoving not unmoved
On whose shoulders sorrows break

On her sleeve one wears a heart
One wields a club

One is a bellbuoy lonesome and responsive

One listens to herself
Talk to me talk about me
Write to me write for me write about me

He lies beside the trunk
Light and dark these and all the other leaves
Rustle and rustle in the angel tree.

The Echoing Stile
for Laura Findlay

Down the green aisle right under Whiteleaf Cross
Where damp wads of beech leaves lie discoloured
At your feet, rotting, smelling good; between
Moss banks where caches of white violets grow:
This way lies the Echoing Stile, long since
Bypassed, ramshackle, facing Bledlow Rise.

No hurry now. Think of the word, only
A syllable or two. Then fill your lungs
And shout, shout! Out of the hill opposite
A voice replies. And then the hill above
Your head picks up the sound, answers, softens
And simplifies it until it dies in air.

So the hills speak. And the stillness after
Is all the greater, reaching right over
The becalmed Vale of Aylesbury. Discover,
Then, all that these hills never proclaim, today
Or any other time (fossil in chalk,
Taste of wild raspberries, the smell of thyme):

Seldom found except by those who search for them,
The secret parts, part of their secret strength.

At Fiesole

Time dies as the light fails.

Tulips of tungsten signal to bats
On their flight-paths; a dog barks
Itself hoarse; the cypresses
Continue to hold their breath.

Whatever happens is elsewhere:
The huddled hilltop towns, below
And indigo; the aureate city.

Through the thyme-rich air hanging
In the dark lane, a pair of fireflies
Dance letters of light . . . they are
Spelling out an enchanted story.

Your breath warm on my breath,
Your breath on the sweet night air.
Time dies as the light fails.

Once upon a time and ever after.

An Approach to the Marsh

The rope is almost paid out here. Bawdeswell
and the ghost of its foul reeve left to stew,
I drive down cool green naves, and soon the lanes
begin to ripple. More pilgrims are shuffled off
to the shrine at Walsingham, and that is an end
to the firm ground of conviction. This is no man's land
that never belongs to earth or sea entirely:
now the flowing barley hemmed by screaming poppies,
a gull perched on a salt-rusted ploughshare
and a gull, a litter of blood-tarred feathers,
festering. A veil of butterflies, opalescent,
dips and quivers and rises, and I come to where
there is no going beyond.
                              Marsh, mud, shifting sand,
creeks sinuous and shining, they look sucked
and rendered almost certain by the sun;
but now and then, and for no evident reason,
rigging yaps, or seabirds shriek at what we cannot
even see, or the sea broadcasts over the marsh . . . .
This bleached boat, that dabber, those children
gathering samphire, leaping over sun-crazed pulks:
the staithe today rests on its August oars;
hard light gives an edge to all that's apparent,
where nothing is what it seems or not for long.

The Old Apple-Tree

'Like hanks of hair,' you said.
'Or nail parings: the tree's well rid
Of them.' Yes, this aching bough
The fruit dragged down, this is misshapen,
This leprous. It all makes sense.
The white wounds do not even ooze . . . .
Then why is it as if the teeth
Were set to my own flesh?

Those eyes in the violet garden –
Pale as mothballs, insides of shells –
No, they are the stumps of limbs
Lopped; creations of the hacksaw.
And what is that the birds sing?
'All growth begins in suffering.'
Look how they shine through night's toils,
The old apple-tree's raised eucharists.

Mary

The angel whirlwind swirls round the cupola.

Beyond the nave's dark fever and the spokes
She concentrates, this girl, half-smiling,
Sits lanced by silence deep as blue drapes.

Grace is acceptance and acceptance grace.

Place of Pilgrimage

Crossing the swollen river, gun-metal and gold
And quivering, breasting the cold current of air
That follows its main course, they come clean to the church

Standing huge and separate in the half-darkness.
The day's pilgrims, the charabancs have departed
And the doors are locked and bolted, all except one.

It is almost warm with the use of believers,
With the power of candles gathered in clusters
Before effigies and images the darkness saddles.

The two of them sit cautious and erect, holding
Their breath, then drawn into the motion
Of this slow, reflective, part-reflecting place.

It has a night-life of its own, unheard by day
And unsuspected. Somewhere in its system
Dripping water ticks; a bat zips out of darkness

Into darkness and all around there are forces
Personified – an entire iconography
They cannot see but sense and almost grasp.

Is that a hand outstretched? This is the moment
You need no longer ask why. No wonder here, then,
Of all places, they think they could trust, could try.

Keys at the door: but they are not locked in
And reckon it would not matter in the least if they were.
A boy hurries in, genuflects unquestioning,

Trims candles here and there, older than his age
In his authority and yet no age at all:
Only the third one, the spirit of the place.

Back to the river they go, and they link hand and hand.
Over them it rises and stands, sure-footed;
In darkness this concentration graced, accountable.

In Dorset and Wiltshire
for Sally and Dick

1.

In the blue hour definitions and distances
Become undecided; the cantering fields
Shimmer with light caught and reluctantly yielded.
First to retreat are the barrows strung out along
The hilltop, cropped and lop-sided but still
To be reckoned with. They gather the darkness
Back into themselves and they emit darkness –
Day's dying reminder – as their builders intended.

2.

If night air thickens and unknowing clouds of mist
Weep and wrap round the cathedral, its floodlights
Seem more powerful; drowned in light, the spire
Rises a second time, a dim delineation
Above itself, disembodied and floating.
Matter illumines spirit, illusion appears miracle:
Darkness disinherited, light begetting light
By which chiefly I see how much I cannot see.

Postcards from Kodai

Kodaikanal is a hill station in the Western Ghats. More than seven thousand feet high, it was developed as a retreat by the English who frequented it during the summer months when life became unbearably hot on the plains.

Here I am once more. Do you remember
the castanets of toads at dusk, thousands
of them? The veil, diaphanous, that drifts
over the glaze of the five-fingered lake?
This will bring it back if anything will.
Colonel Edgcumbe is here again and sends
regards – we two are the last survivors.

•

Have you ever stood higher than the clouds
and watched them smoking, lifting from valleys?
This is the eyrie of the Western Ghats.
From the verandah of this bungalow
I can survey the whole apparent world,
everything, my dear, trapped in place or time,
hazy or shining. Godlike, powerless!

•

Down at the Carlton the new head waiter
is called Joseph! Is that a requirement
for the post? They still fold all the napkins
in unexpected ways and trick them out
with wildflowers. A log fire in the grate
and, outside, the cool air close with pinesmoke,
the improving smell of eucalyptus
(only this would seem the least out of place
in an Alpine resort). Dear old Kodai!
There are changes here, but not as elsewhere.

•

You'd laugh, Emily. The Carlton Hotel –
I went there for tea with Colonel Edgcumbe –
still has the books we combed through as children:
Just Patty, *True Tilda* and *Bawbee Jock*.
Does that ring a bell or two? They're wrapped now

in parcel paper, and kept behind glass.
As if they were quite irreplaceable.

●

Big changes in the air at the golf club!
A 'high water rise tank and sump' have been
installed; they mean to replace all the browns
with greens. What was good enough for us . . .
But no, they must always go one better.
It all seems a dreadful waste of money.
Are these the highest golf links anywhere?
I asked the new secretary but he does
not know. Typical! Hope this card gets through!

●

Light is a generous discoverer.
Like God, it finds itself. The sleeping lake
wakes, stretches, slips into its newfound shape
as if all its life had been the darkness
of dream and illusion. A countenance
liquid, empty, impassive; one bird sings . . . .

●

I can't quite explain it but I feel free
to ride my own tides: it is a certain
glory in all my thoughts and emotions,
the ego's representatives. They are
my coat of many colours on this earth.
The same force that fathers inhibition
and denial changes course within me:
here I can become the song of myself.

●

You'd think little or nothing of the sound
of rain falling on outstretched leaves, falling
from leaf to leaf. You hear it every day
almost. But this soft rainmusic, my dear,
always at my ear with how it will be,
how it was: this is really why I come
to this dreaming hill station. I suppose
it is the nearest I will get to home.

Mosquito

Silent fizzer, sting white in the sunlight,
arrowing through air-tides –
                              no sooner said
than you suspect and circle a target
or drift sideways into shadow, unassailable.

A splinter of man's own irritation,
you were here in the beginning,
grinding your teeth.
                        Not much more
than your own appetite, you pick locks
as you please and are skilled at escape.
You weave out of corners, fade before lunges,
Houdini of the darkening straits.

But you come back for more. Disengagement
cannot be your tactic.
                       This is a war-game
and ends only with blood's scintilla.
Or no, does not end at all. Abroad,
and under the fan: the shades of your autograph
walk all day across my prickling skin.

Three Ways of Pinking Ivory

'By this I am telling it should be
Duty elephant. Jungle wallahs daub
The young tusks unless it comes to pass
Into the jungle in case it is stolen.
All the daubs become deep stains, isn't it!
Magenta, pink, this one very pink dream.
Yes sir, yes sir, anything sir likes sir.'

'All you need is a bowl of rose water.
Dip in your ivory, dunk it there
For two three days. Prepare another bowl
If you are insisting on a darker hue,
Like this little one is Sarasvati.
You prefer this ivory, white as bone?
Yes sir, yes sir, anything sir likes sir.'

'Acquire it. And wait. You can do nothing
To hurry it any more than you can
Hurry time, or arrest it. This bracelet
Is a bit old, at least ten years. It has
Life of its own, no, and as you yellow
With years, it will yellow also. Or pink.
Yes sir, yes sir, anything sir likes sir.'

Note on the Language Riots in Tamil Nadu, 1967

'They poured kerosene over their own bodies
And set them on fire.
No, there was no end to their spring of anger
Coiled in a gyre.

They made a mighty image of a Hindi-speaker
From wire and sacking,
Wheeled it through the shouting streets, gave it
A slipper-whacking.'

South-West Monsoon

The eyelids of a dreaming man; the subtle
Swift movement of a trout into shadow
Or is it the white shift of water itself.
Ripple and flicker, flicker and ripple,
The far-off lightning makes its connections
In the skull. It is very peaceful.
There are no reports. As if the war
Were conducted tonight on some other front.

    As it was then . . . a malt in my hand
    (Especially shipped for the English Club),
    A trichinopoli, and a verandah,
    Not an infernal pink-and-muggy room.
    Boys waiting in the shadows . . . damn them!
    They even move like shadows of themselves.
    I'll sit in my cane before this flickering
    Screen, prepared for what may not ever come.

Dazed brass gleams like a fallen moon:
A girl with a waterpot on her head
Walks her liquid walk up the rustling road,
She is sizing the world under her soles.
If she stopped to think, she could tell
Nothing has changed since the beginning.
Aching limbs, sweet water from the well,
Aching limbs . . . . A mongrel howls . . . .

    Every four seconds the needle dances
    And the scape is scalded. Plantains leap
    Out of Dravidian dark, the compound of huts,
    The coarse thatching of coconut palm, old men
    At the thresholds. No one moves.
    No one has ever moved. At times like this
    You could stuff the whole bloody scene
    And no one would know the difference.

The cool tones of the wind's announcement:
The rain, sheet rain, smacks the glazed face
Of the hotel. In a hundred frames
The sheet glass rocks and holds. The world contracts.
Beyond the panes not even one smear of light,
A kerosene star; the whole compound wiped out.
A Noah's Ark full of grateful prisoners,
The hotel buckets into the darkness.

    Yes, I remember . . . the bluster, the dark wave
    That hoisted us on to its shoulder.
    'Batten the hatches! Batten the hatches!'
    Nothing to do but sit and sweat it out,
    The lizards watching the dancing mosquitoes;
    The eyes of the boys, molten, secretive;
    The winking eye of malt; eye of the storm;
    The bungalow bleared, a drowning eye.

Seep and trickle first, pool under the window,
A wound superficial and easily dressed;
But then water wells under the crooked door
And boys hurry in with cloths and containers.
The breach is made, though, the body imperilled.
Fabric and form, what is not at risk
In time of these rains that hammer at the house
Of the active man, the house of the head?

At St Gregory's Minster, Kirkdale
'This is day's Sun marker at every tide'

And then you led me through the wash
of primroses and faintly-coloured flowers
to see the sundial on St Gregory's.

I am so lonely. Sometimes I talk to the cows.

Pale sun glossed your face. Under violet eyes
the shadows seemed only tissue-deep,
and I never guessed this was your last tide.

Neenie
in memory of F. I. M. Crossley-Holland

Under the cowl, out on Scolt Head,
The swell and swash are inching their way back.
The water picks up pebbles, razor shells,
Birds' small bleached bones and witches' purses;
It toys with them, cries over them,
And the legendary wave embraces them.

The tide returning: each wave and whisker,
Everything forged into one force,
A fusion with one meaning and purpose.
But I think you are going further,
Ancient shuffler, at the fire now, flushed
By this last blaze before going to bed.

Out of the dark they come at a knobbled wave,
Processions unblemished and undeterred
By time's strictures. Here is the hall
At Oakwell: *The chimney always roars like this;*
Frank is still up in the organ gallery,
Puffing his cigar, blowing out another hymn.

The wind, more wind, and the cottage
Rocks like a boat, quite safe, out at sea.
Remember the train we took up to Wengen
When you were six and I was sixty?
It rocks, nurse, it rocks. I love this nursery.
Kevin, have you met my pregnant sister?

And now there is rain, ripping against the window
(Long since painted into its frame)
Behind the curtain of faded red velvet.
What will become of the passion flowers?
Still, the borders of this tapestry are teeming
With forget-me-nots. I had three proposals . . . .

It goes on and on. You make associations
As children and poets do, bony fingers
Clamped to the sill now, eyes watering:
Not only the tide flowing and gathering up
As it goes, not only time defused,
But for itself a parade of whatever mattered

And for whatever reason, a statement
Risen clear of interest and argument.
I listen and think you are telling something
Greater than its parts, a breath and sum
Of life itself, the ego dispossessed.
Grandmother, sleep, and sleep in peace.

After Your Death

1.

Poppy-heads on pew-ends,
The wind without, and in the porch,

All life gone, this one bleached leaf
Like lace you would have loved.

2.

The sweet bending rushes know,
Bending low, jostling and whispering.

The gulls know, each pair describing
Figures in the air, wheeling and screaming.

The sky knows, wearing your favourite
Colours: pale blue and blue-green, indigo.

The stones know, shoulder to shoulder,
Locked in silence and diminishing.

The creek knows. The water knows
And ebbs, ebbs before it can return.

3.

Heart-throb's foxed photograph;
Snowdrop; birdsong.

Unearth and airborne:
Death's compounds, life's couplings.

A Wreath
*in memory of Edmund who was born and died on
1 June 1976*

The furled cypress contains it. The breathless yew. Hulks of elms all over England.

A trail of shadows, everywhere, in the oblique sunlight. Who does not accept them. Who is not even grateful for them?

But when the bud . . . .

*

Not one sound can be undone. It is part of the harmony of the gong.

Look at the water. It sways, catches chips of light, flashes, sways.

Yet snared by time, all of us, that part of us . . . .

Not one stone, one leaf, one flame, one breath. Whatever begins is eternal.

*

Where he lies now a moonstone lies, one with flint and chert and every granule of earth.

And the darkness comprehendeth it not . . . .

A moonstone on her throbbing hand. Light in the stone, life's pointer. Brother of the hawthorn, the wood-anemone, the breathing iridescent universe.

Cassandra

It's cheese what causes dreams, innit?
At night, I mean. That's what me mum
says, anyhow. I was thirty-two weeks,
well, thirty-two or thirty-four,
you know, depending.... Anyway I got
back in after a wee, right,
and the HB tablets I'd forgotten before,
and I do remember it was raining
and Ron was snoring like a bloody pig.
Must've dozed off and this dame, this dame
sorta stood over me, know what I mean.
Dripping. Ab-sol-ute-ly soaking!
Well, I had a butchers, and she stared
straight back, a gloomy sorta chevy.
She fixed me with her eyes, right,
all mournful, and says in a holler voice,
'Edith!' 'Pleased to meet yer,' I says.
'I'm Cassandra,' she moans. 'Cassandra.
I need shelter. Gimme shelter.'
And then, in a bit, 'Let me come home.'

Anyway, the name sorta stuck, right,
like the Queen Mum's fishbone.
So when she was born that's what I called her.
Didn't I, ye-es, yes I did!
Ron said I was a nutter. Barm-y!
'Whaddya want a name like that for?
Cassandra! Poor little scrap!
Bloody hell!' All that sorta crap.
'Yer can stick it up yer Khyber,' I says.
'Up yours, Cassandra!' says he.
But what gives me the heeby-jeebies
is that second dream. Her again,
dressed in a kinda sheet thing,
know what I mean. Enough to freeze
yer cobblers! She sorta drifted
over me, drifted, right, and whispered,
'Edith!' I couldn't say nothing,

not in my dream, I was that choked.
'Thanks for that, Edith,' she moans.
'You did better an you know, girl . . . .'

Dragon
for Gillian

Swirling fire-drake astride the northern skies,
Fafnir, Knucker and Serpent of Henham,
Muckle Mester Stoor Worm and Civic Snap:

Bless your sister sprung in human form,
Let this girl with a storm of flaming hair
Be abundant as a dragon from the orient,

A house-guardian, a bringer of rain.

Sigurd and Beowulf, George, Carantoc,
Seigneur de Hambrye, Shonks and Assipattle:
Turn protectors now with your massive shields

And your spiked war-gear, your poison and fire.
She will be ruler of the inner kingdom.
I say she is worthy of all your care

And the light armour of a poet's words.

Deliverance

My skull cracks open.
Look at the birds,
look at the birds released, a spray,
a fantail flowering.

First the lark, up, out and away,
hitting top C like a piano-tuner;
the humming-bird, the mocking-bird,
the bird of paradise;
look at the sparrows and pipits;
the gull like a longing,
sea-ranger never satisfied;
ravens, two of them,
heavy with the weight of Thought and Memory.

This is the day of the rainbow,
the bird with a twig in its beak.
At last, when least expected,
this is the great escape.
Uncontainable
they fly, purposive, interweaving;
they mingle and they sing,
and I shall not go mad.

Death and the Maiden

How soul from body slowly does unwind
Until we are pure spirit at the end.
ROETHKE

The old man said:

I sauntered through a glade,
a long natural green neck
between sweet-smelling pines,
so thoroughly at ease,
as if I had fallen into step
with the speed of the world.
There was no path until I made it,
brushing the downy maidenhair;
listening to a cuckoo,
two-toned and mournful, insisting:
Remember, if only you could;
remember, if only you could
remember . . . .
               The glade swelled
into a pasture, and that dipped
and rose, concave,
crossed with sheep runs,
knobbly with many outcrops,
towards the sheer rock and the snowline,
still hanging back.
               Coming on
that open, intercostal land,
nudged by the jumpy wind,
I quickened my step. But still
there were flowers under my feet,
small colonies, keeping their heads down,
yellow and yellowy-white.
I followed a trickling watercourse
and beside it, in the turf,
amongst rabbits' droppings,
found strange prints, small
and heart-shaped; it was as if Pan

were somewhere about. Then,
higher up, where the incline
reared into an escarpment,
there was a band of camomile,
creeping and unimpressionable.
Over the top, the wind grabbed
and rattled me; I faced
a thousand jaws, a grey
and silver rocky sea.
                    I kept
to the watercourse but now
it was dry. There were ferns
underfoot, last year's,
orange and crackling;
and, on the pitted and mottled rock,
untender bristly lichen.
That was where I paused;
for a while I rested
in a scoop of stone, and when
I closed my eyes, I remember
there was little darkness, peaceful
and uniform; rather, something composite
as the granite I reclined on —
shifting sombre clouds,
sudden glints and flashes.
Later I set out again
and, under a boast of rock,
discovered a holly tree in blossom
and full berry, both out of season.
Glossy, ancient, almost unaware
of the wind, it stood
expecting no change.
White as the lily flower . . .
Red as any blood . . . .
The words went round my head,
first welcome, then unwanted,
repeated and repeated,
until they were nothing but sounds.

I clambered out of that jagged glen,
glanced down at the silent holly,
and then the snow summit reared
over my shoulders.
                I scrambled
over scree, and, as always,
the seemingly straightforward contained
surprises, platforms, hollows, creases,
new truths in the lie of the land.
And so, as if by chance, I came —
just where the fissures and daylong shadows
were lined with snow — to a small
green terrace and a small hut,
unmarked on any map,
unannounced and unexpected.
                        When winter
howls, and darkness draws on,
and brings fierce hailstorms
from the north to frighten men . . . .
Curious and spring-heeled again,
I came to the threshold,
and there I heard it clearly,
music within.
                She lay on trestles,
dressed in loose white linen,
her unlined face, her fingers, her feet
luminous in the gloom;
and her moon-hair was so long
it coursed to the floor
like a distant, arrested waterfall.
She lay so still, so undisturbed,
it was as if she had never moved.
They were grouped around her,
four musicians; what they played
seemed a rage of contradictions,
hesitations, apparent solutions,
a celebration almost of conflict.

But then from within, within the maelstrom,
far under the waves,
combining opposites, gain and waste,
emerged this one undeniable song,
this unreasonable pure recognition
I sing and you sing . . . .

If Only the Wind

If only the wind would come down from the trees....
Have I heard these words, or words like these,
Or lifted them from some half-buried layer?
That haunting sense: the inexplicably familiar.

Suppose in the dark garden I wait:
When was it ever as easy as that?
Not the least pulse in the hanging air,
Neither damp grass nor the chaste leaves stir.

Yet nearly at hand there seems to go
So much I almost know or did once know.
The topmost branches sing and swing at ease.
If only the wind would come down from the trees.

Moon-Child

I am several and I am one,
Between my horns I carry the light of the sun.

I am not crescent or quarter only;
I want as you want. You will see me wholly

Not tonight but one night.
Wrestle with your own ghosts, embody them, make light.

'But the frost, the pestle, the almost lost . . . .'
You are time's child, this is the cost.

But the flow, too, is our shared weather.
What can we do not done together?

I will rise full, the several one that never dies.
Wait. Raise your eyes.